Daddy's Expressions of Love

Barry Buchignani

Daddy's Expressions of Love

Inspired by my amazing Lola Grace

Daddy's Love

I love when you stare back at me
when you're lying in your bed.
I love holding you in my arms and
rubbing your little head.

I love bouncing you on my knees and
watching you roll on the floor.
I love giving you hugs and kisses
because that's what dads are for.

I love when we eat together and
play with all your toys.
I love when we have nap time and
when we're making lots of noise.

I love that you are so curious
and look at everything.
I love it when your little hands
tug on Daddy's bangs.

I love when it is bedtime so we can say our prayers.
I love that you are going to sleep
without any worries or cares.

I love to watch you lie and sleep
because Daddy loves you so,
And Daddy loves knowing we'll
do it again tomorrow.

Blessed

Too many blessings is how I feel.
When I look at you, my love is so real.

I'm blessed with vision to see your face,
To see you smile. The view is great.

To watch you grow and watch you change,
To watch you play and live each day,

To watch you crawl, stand tall, and take steps,
My love for you is beyond the rest.

You're my angel. You're the best.
You are why I am so blessed.

I am blessed with hands to hold you close,
To caress your cheek, and poke your nose,

To rub your belly and stroke your head
Before I lay you down for bed.

To grab your finger and tickle your feet
And squeeze your tush; you are so sweet.

With these hands I help you pick up your mess.
You are why I am so blessed.

I am blessed with ears to hear your sounds.
Your little giggles echo all around.

To hear your squeaks and your first words,
I'm blessed because they are not unheard.

To hear your cries, laughs, and sneezes,
My love for you is how God loves Jesus.

To hear you sigh in peace as you
lay across my chest,
You are why Daddy is so blessed.

One of a kind

Say your prayers. Let's get ready for bed.
Close your eyes. Lay down your head.

It's time to relax your body and unwind.
Peaceful thoughts appear dancing in your mind.

Let your imagination go. What will you find?
That you are very special and one of a kind.

There is no limit to what you can achieve.
You can be a princess or a star on TV.

You can cure diseases. You may be the missing key.
You can do anything in life. All
you must do is believe.

You are going to fly in life like
the eagles high above.
You have introduced Daddy to
a special kind of love.

It's an indescribable feeling with
its own appearance.
I wish every person in the world
could have this experience.

It's a natural love that happens
without even trying.
You're surrounded by the Lord's
blessings—there is no denying.

So sleep, little angel, like Jesus in the manger,
Without any worries or signs of danger.

Favorite

You're my favorite prayer that
fills my heart with joy.
You're the calm I need
when I get annoyed.

When my day is dark, you're my vibrant light.
You're my shining star that brightens up the night.

You're my favorite song to which
I always hum along.
You're my favorite scent, like a flower in the lawn.

You are like a sunrise, a beauty to my eyes.
You're my positivity that tells
my negatives goodbye.

You're my inspiration. You always give me hope,
And when I need a laugh, you're my favorite joke.

You're my favorite movie that I
watch over and over again.
The love I have for you goes
beyond a ten out of ten.

You're my favorite blanket I cuddle on the bed.
You're my favorite thought dancing in my head.

You're my favorite creation, more
precious than the world.
You're my whole life. You're Daddy's little girl.

Barry Buchignani has always enjoyed writing poems for fun about people and situations in his life. It wasn't until his daughter was born that she became the focal point of his poetry. He loves spending time writing poetry and being with friends and family in Lexington Kentucky.